The Green Dragons

Story by Sonny Mulheron

Illustrations by Meredith Thomas

Annie loved soccer.
Her brother Sam was older
and bigger than she was,
and he played soccer
for the Green Dragons
every Saturday morning.

Annie wanted to play for them, too,
but Dad said,
"The Green Dragons are all
older than you.
You can't play for them,
but you can come along and watch."

So, every Saturday morning,
    when Dad took Sam
        and his friend Dylan to play soccer,
Annie went along to watch the game.

Annie stood next to Dad
at the side of the soccer field.
When the Green Dragons had the ball
and ran up the field,
she cheered and shouted,
and ran along the sideline to keep up.

"I can run as fast as they can,"
said Annie.

"There's more to soccer
than just running," said Dad.
"There's dribbling and passing
and kicking."

4

"I can do those things,"
said Annie.

"You can't do **all** of them,"
said Dad.

For two Saturdays in a row,
the Green Dragons **lost**!

"We will have to practice more,"
said the coach.

So, on most evenings,
when Dad came home from work,
he took Sam and Dylan
to the park for a quick game.

Annie played, too.
Soon she was really good
at kicking the ball
while she was running.

Sam could do it all better,
but he said,
"You're catching on, Annie."

One Thursday, when Annie went
to soccer practice with Sam,
the coach let her join in.
"You're young," said the coach,
"but you're starting to be
a good kicker. And you can run."

The next Saturday, Annie and Dad
went to watch the Green Dragons
play the Gold Tigers.

With only two minutes to go,
the score was tied. It was 3 to 3.

Then Dylan fell and twisted his ankle!

The Gold Tigers' coach said,
"Do you have another player
who can go in?"

The Green Dragons' coach said, "No."
But then he said,
"Hang on! Wait a minute.
There's Annie. She could play."

The Gold Tigers' coach smiled
when he saw how small Annie was.
"You can put **her** in," he said.

Annie grabbed a green shirt
and rushed onto the field.

Annie ran along beside Sam.
She watched another team member
pass the ball to Sam.
She watched Sam dribble the ball
with his feet.

Sam ran for the goal, but a tall girl
playing defense for the Gold Tigers
was getting closer and closer.
If she kicked the ball away from Sam,
time would run out
before they could score.

Sam looked around for someone
to pass the ball to.
Annie was beside him,
and he kicked her the ball
just in time.

"Run!" shouted Sam.
"Kick the ball into the goal!"

"**Kick it!**" shouted the coach.

"Kick!" shouted Dad.

Annie kicked harder than
she had ever kicked before.

Annie kicked the ball into the goal
just beyond the goalie's reach.

"A goal!" yelled the Green Dragons.
"Annie scored a goal!
She can play for us **any** time."